DATE DUE		

597.96   Patton, Don.   106015351
PAT

Pythons

LAKE SUPERIOR ELEMENTARY LMC
6200 E 3RD STREET SUPERIOR WI

628308 01595   12597C   004

PYTHONS

PYTHONS

DON PATTON

THE CHILD'S WORLD

Somewhere in the middle of the moist rainforest, a large snake hangs from the branch of a tree. As the snake hangs there, swaying slightly back and forth, it looks like any of the hundreds of vines in the surrounding trees. A wild pig moves along a path through the forest, unaware of the danger waiting ahead. As the pig passes beneath the snake, the cold-blooded reptile detects the pig's warm body. The snake drops from its perch, wrapping itself tightly around the startled pig. In a few minutes it is over: the pig is dead and the snake has a meal. The large reptile swallows the pig whole and slowly moves into the brush to rest and digest its meal.

The python is one of the world's largest snakes. There are twenty species of pythons, ranging in size from the *Asian reticulated python* (thirty-three feet long and over 300 pounds!) to the *ball python* (only eight feet long and four to seven pounds). Each species shows a different pattern in the coloring of its smooth scales. These patterns allow the snakes to blend into their environments. Scientists call these kinds of color patterns *camouflage*. Camouflage helps an animal hide.

Pythons move from place to place in much the same way a caterpillar or a centipede does. The snake inches its way forward by moving its belly scales. The belly scales act like the legs of a caterpillar, anchoring the animal in one spot and pulling it forward in another. This type of snake movement is called *creeping*.

10

Pythons are not poisonous snakes. They capture their prey by hiding in trees or brush and surprising animals that stray too near, using their sense of smell to determine whether the animal would make a good meal. The snake's tongue flicks in and out quickly, bringing with it the scent of the surrounding air. In the roof of its mouth, the snake has a small scent organ called, *Jacobson's organ*, that is far more sensitive than the human nose.

Once the snake decides to attack, it relies on its heat receptors to help locate its meal. The snake lunges forward and grasps its prey by the head, coiling tightly around the victim and squeezing tighter every time the captured animal breathes out. This process is called *constriction*. Eventually, the prey is unable to breathe and dies. The python must be very powerful to kill its prey in this manner.

A python can swallow animals larger than its head! Instead of the long fangs found in poisonous snakes, pythons have many small, sharp teeth. The teeth hold the food tightly as the snake unlocks its jaw and stretches its mouth. The python then contracts muscles that draw the prey further and further down its throat and into its stomach. After the snake swallows a large animal, it has a visible lump that slowly moves through its digestive system and toward its tail.

Pythons feed mostly on small mammals and birds. Rodents such as mice and rats are the most common prey. Usually, a python eats many small animals rather than a few large ones. A large python, though, may sometimes eat animals weighing 100 pounds! Humans are much too large and quick to be common prey for pythons, so although python attacks on humans do occur, they are very rare. A person faces a much greater chance of being hit by lightning than being attacked by a python!

Of the 2,500 species of snakes in the world, pythons are one of the most primitive. Millions of year ago, snakes developed from reptiles that moved underground and lost the need for legs. Pythons still have portions of their ancestral hip bones, however, and horny claws where their legs were once located.

The environment or area in which an animal lives is known as its *habitat*. Most pythons live in tropical rainforest habitats. These areas are full of trees and bushes the snakes can use for camouflage. Tropical rainforests are found in Africa, Australia, Central America, South America, India, Southeast Asia, and the East Indies. Other areas that a few species of pythons inhabit include dry deserts, high mountains, and grassy plains.

Pythons mate in the spring, and the female lays her eggs in the early summer. She lays approximately one hundred eggs, called a *clutch*, and coils her body around them to help warm and protect the growing babies. The sun also helps to warm the developing eggs. The mother stays with the eggs continuously for two months.

Using a small sharp spine, called an egg tooth, each small snake breaks a hole in its egg and begins to hatch. From this point on, the baby python is on its own, learning to catch food and defend itself from predators. A baby reticulated python may be twenty to twenty-six inches long at hatching and weigh only four ounces.

Pythons continue to grow throughout their entire lives. How fast they grow depends on their success in capturing food. During its first year, a young python may grow to three times its original length. The rate of growth slows as the animal gets older but, unlike in humans and other mammals, never really stops. Large snakes like pythons may live for twenty or thirty years!

Many people fear pythons and other snakes, but these animals play an important role in nature. Pythons consume thousands of tons of rodents annually, keeping the rodent population at stable levels. Rodents damage farm crops and spread many human diseases. If left uncontrolled, their populations would soar, causing heavy damage and disease. By controlling rodent populations, pythons help reduce human starvation and sickness. By understanding these giant snakes and realizing the important role they play in nature, perhaps humans can replace their fear with respect.

INDEX

PHOTO RESEARCH
Jim Rothaus / James R. Rothaus & Associates

PHOTO EDITOR
Robert A. Honey / Seattle

PHOTO CREDITS
TOM STACK & ASSOCIATES / David M. Dennis: cover,31
TOM STACK & ASSOCIATES / D.G. Barker: 2,8,22,24
Norbert Wu: 4,11,13
Michael Cardwell: 7
UNICORN STOCK PHOTOS: Jay Foreman: 14
TOM STACK & ASSOCIATES / John Cancalosi: 17
WIDE WORLD PHOTOS: 18,21
TOM STACK & ASSOCIATES / Joe McDonald: 27
Dan Polin: 28

Library of Congress Cataloging-in-Publication Data
Patton, Don.
Pythons / Don Patton.
p. cm.
Includes index.
ISBN 1-56766-180-7
1. Pythons – Juvenile literature
[1. Pythons.] [2. Snakes.]
I. Title.
QL666.O63P38 1995   95-7388
597.96 – dc20   CIP
                                                    AC